Other Books from FranklinCovey

The 7 Habits of Happy Kids

The 4 Disciplines of Execution

The Speed of Trust

The 7 Habits of Highly Effective People

*The 6 Most Important Decisions You'll Ever Make:
A Guide for Teens*

Principle-Centered Leadership

First Things First

The Leader in Me

The 3rd Alternative

The 8th Habit

The Wisdom and Teachings of Stephen R. Covey

Let's Get Real or Let's Not Play

Great Work, Great Career

Smart Trust

The 7 Habits of Highly Effective Families

The 7 Habits of Highly Effective Teens

Life Matters

What Matters Most

The 10 Natural Laws of Successful Time and Life Management

The Power Principle

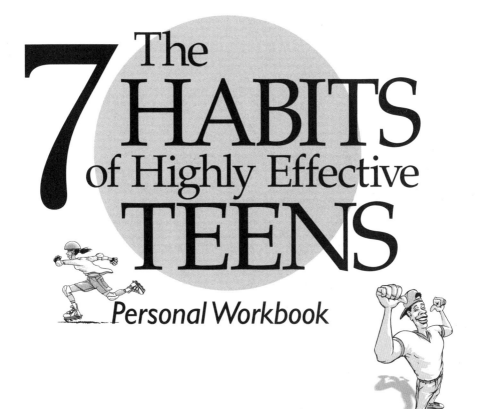

The 7 HABITS of Highly Effective TEENS

Personal Workbook

Sean Covey

TOUCHSTONE
New York   London   Toronto   Sydney   New Delhi

Touchstone
An Imprint of Simon & Schuster, Inc.
1230 Avenue of the Americas
New York, NY 10020

For information about special discounts for bulk purchases, please contact Simon & Schuster Special Sales at 1-866-506-1949 or business@simonandschuster.com.

The Simon & Schuster Speakers Bureau can bring authors to your live event. For more information or to book an event, contact the Simon & Schuster Speakers Bureau at 1-866-248-3049 or visit our website at www.simonspeakers.com.

Interior design by Ruth Lee-Mui
Cover photograph © Yusuf Sarlar/E+/Getty Images

Manufactured in the United States of America

10   9

Library of Congress Cataloging-in-Publication data is available.

ISBN 978-1-4767-6468-9

Get in
the Habit

THEY MAKE YOU OR BREAK YOU

What Exactly Are Habits?  ead pages 5–6 of the *Teens* book. The 7 Habits of Highly Effective Teens are:

Habit 1: **Be Proactive—**
Take responsibility for your life.

Habit 2: **Begin with the End in Mind—**
Define your mission and goals in life.

Habit 3: **Put First Things First—**
Prioritize, and do the most important things first.

Habit 4: **Think Win-Win—**
Have an everyone-can-win attitude.

Habit 5: **Seek First to Understand, Then to Be Understood—**
Listen to people sincerely.

Habit 6: **Synergize—**
Work together to achieve more.

Habit 7: **Sharpen the Saw—**
Renew yourself regularly.

> We first make
> our habits,
> then our habits
> make us.
>
> —ENGLISH POET

Habits are things you do repeatedly. But most of the time you are hardly aware you do them. They happen when you're on cruise control. Depending on what they are, your

1

habits will either make you or break you. You become what you repeatedly do. Luckily, you can outgrow the bad ones, or shake them off. Remember: you are stronger than your habits.

Let's look at some of the good habits you have in your life right now. (Good habits include things such as working out regularly, being a trustworthy friend, or being on time for homeroom.)

Think About Your Habits

Four of my really great habits are:

1. _____

2. _____

3. _____

4. _____

The reason I keep these habits in my life is:

The good results I get from having each good habit are: (For example: I have good posture, and I think it makes me appear more confident.)

Habits aren't always positive; they can be good, bad, or just neutral. Some habits I have that are neutral (they're neither good nor bad— they're just habits) are: (For example: I pour milk in the bowl before I pour in the cereal.)

Now let's list some habits you're not so proud of. Complete the statements that follow:

Right now, my worst habits are:

The reason I have these bad habits is:

I've had these bad habits for (days, weeks, years?):

The bad results I get from having these bad habits are: (For example: I keep texting during class, which means I don't take notes and get lower grades then I should.)

From my list of bad habits above, the one habit I would like to change the most is:

Change the Bad to Good

On the table below, fill in the habits that you named above. Keep this table handy during the upcoming week and use it as a tool to help you remember to change your bad habits to good ones.

BAD HABIT I WANT TO CHANGE	GOOD HABIT I WANT TO REPLACE IT WITH

In School:

1. _____   1. _____

2. _____   2. _____

3. _____   3. _____

With My Family:

1. _____   1. _____

2. _____   2. _____

3. _____   3. _____

With My Friends:

1. _____   1. _____

2. _____   2. _____

3. _____   3. _____

Other:

1. _____   1. _____

2. _____   2. _____

3. _____   3. _____

A cool thing about the 7 Habits is how they build on each other. It's a progression—just like learning arithmetic before calculus, memorizing the alphabet before learning to spell, or programming a website before launching it online. Trees grow this way, too; they put down solid roots before the trunk, branches, or leaves begin to grow.

Fill in the habits on the tree that follows from what you have learned so far.

I pull myself out of it by: (Describe your actions.)

I have someone I can talk to. True or false?

That person is:

He or she listens to me by: (How does he or she listen?)

He or she is easy to talk to because:

Who is someone else you can talk to besides friends or family (therapist, counselor, teacher)?

- **LAUGH OR YOU'LL CRY**

After all is said and done, there is one key ingredient to keeping your heart healthy and strong. Just laugh, loud and long and clear. (Isn't that what Mary Poppins said?)

Did you know that by the time you reach kindergarten, you laugh about three hundred times a day? In contrast, the typical adult laughs a measly seventeen times a day. Where are you? Three hundred times a day or seventeen?

> Life loves to be taken by the lapel and told, "I'm with you, kid. Let's go."
> —MAYA ANGELOU

Laughter also promotes good health and speedy recoveries, so it's not just good for your heart—it's good for your body!

If you're not laughing much now, do something about it. Start a humor collection—collect funny stories, YouTube videos, memes, and jokes. Remember to never let your laughter become unkind or at the expense of others. Learn to laugh at yourself when strange things happen to you or when you do something kinda stupid.

Look for Ways to Laugh

These things always make me laugh:

My three favorite funny movies/TV shows/online videos/memes are:

1. _____

2. _____

3. _____

My favorite line from these that just cracks me up is:

My favorite comedian/comedienne is:

Something that made me laugh today was:

> Laughter is the
> shortest distance
> between two people.
>
> —VICTOR BORGE

Care for Your Soul

Your soul is your center. Within it lies your deepest convictions and values. It's the source for purpose, meaning, and inner peace. Habit 7: Sharpen the Saw teaches that sharpening the saw in the spiritual area of life means taking time to renew and awaken that inner self.

THAT'S IT! WE'RE SWITCHING TO NICKELODEON.

What would happen to someone who drank only energy drinks and ate only chocolate for several years? What would he or she look like and feel like after a while? Would the result be any different if you fed your soul trash for several years? You're not only what you eat, you're also what you listen to, read, and see. Maybe more important than what goes into your body is what goes into your soul.

Your soul is a very private area of your life. You can feed it in many ways. Here are some ideas shared by others:

- Meditating
- Expressing my creativity through art, music, or technology
- Working with my hands, for example cooking
- Listening to inspirational music
- Serving others
- Praying
- Being in nature

Feed Your Soul the Good Stuff

I feed my soul by: (Describe your actions.)

Some new things I would like to add are:

Am I feeding my soul nutrients or junk? Am I putting things into my soul that I really don't want in there? Some of these things are:

You choose what you're going to feed your soul with—don't let the world decide for you. The media has a light side and a dark side.

The kind of media I am exposing my soul to is:

The media exposure that I find harmful to my moods is:

I think this happens because:

Social media connects you to people all over the world. But if you just go on to check out how everyone else is having more fun than you, it'll probably make you feel pretty isolated. If you ever need a break from Facebook, Twitter, Instagram, etc., just disconnect for a few days—you can always go back to it.

How does using social media make me feel? How can I use it more wisely?

Rate Your Ability to Care for Your Soul
Check off the items that describe you:

❑ I have defined what my values are and I plan to live my life accordingly.

❑ I have created my mission statement. I rely on it to give vision to my purpose in life.

❑ I renew each day through meditation, prayer, study, or reflection.

❑ I frequently spend time in a place where I can spiritually renew, such as in nature, a synagogue, a chapel, a mosque, or a temple.

❏ I live with integrity and honor.

❏ I keep my heart open to others and their beliefs.

❏ I take a stand or tell the truth, even when opposed by others.

❏ I frequently serve others without expectations of a returned favor.

❏ I can identify which things in life I can change and which things I cannot. I let go of the things I cannot change.

● **GETTING BACK TO NATURE**

Habit 7: Sharpen the Saw explains that there is something magical about getting into nature. Even if you live in a downtown area far removed from rivers, mountains, or beaches, there is usually a park nearby, or some nature a drive or train ride away. Getting into nature is a great way to nourish your soul.

> The soul was never put in the body to stand still.
> —JOHN WEBSTER

Make a Date with Nature

1. Read the Getting Back to Nature section that appears on page 235 of the *Teens* book.
2. Choose one of these activities to help you get in touch with nature this week:
   - Plant some flowers, vegetables, or herbs.
   - Weed a flower bed or vegetable garden every day this week.
   - Mow or water the lawn once this week.
   - Watch the sunset and sunrise and notice their differences.
   - Look on your calendar to see the date of the next full moon. Schedule time to look at it.
   - Watch for the different phases of the moon, and recognize how each phase affects the way the moon looks.
   - Get involved in some environmental groups in your community and learn how you and your family can be more eco-friendly.
   - Take a walk in your neighborhood. Notice the types of trees you see, the birds that fly there, the insects that crawl around, and the flowers that grow.
   - Go to the zoo. Choose two different animals to observe, and watch them for fifteen minutes each. Identify the differences between them.

HABIT 7

- Compare a river to a lake. Recognize the differences between them.
- Identify different states of water (for example, ice, clouds, etc.). Find examples of these in your community.
- Go to the hills or mountains near you, and identify natural habitats.

The activity I chose was: _____

My experience with nature made me feel: (Describe your experience.)

• GET REAL

When you think about renewal do you think, "Get real. Who has the time? I'm at school all day, I have activities after school, and I study all night." There is a time for everything—a time to be balanced and a time to be imbalanced. Imbalance happens, and you will have times when you don't get enough sleep, eat too much junk food, and spend too much time studying or working to get any exercise. But there are also times for renewal.

If you go too hard for too long, you won't think as clearly, you'll be cranky, and you'll begin to lose perspective. You think you don't have time for building relationships, getting exercise, spending time getting in touch with your soul; but in reality, you don't have time not to.

> Balance is the key to success in all things. Do not neglect your mind, body, or spirit. Invest time and energy in all of them equally—it will be the best investment you ever make, not just for your life but for whatever is to follow.
>
> —TANYA WHEWAY

Regain Your Balance

I have been out of balance lately. True or False?

Why or why not?

I can get back into a more stable and balanced routine by doing:

Believe it or not, just doing this workbook is helping you create more balance in life—if you've done the exercises and the Baby Steps, if you've taken time to feed your body, your mind, your heart, and your soul! Good job!

Choose one or two Baby Steps you can do. Share your experiences with someone else, or write your experiences and learnings here.

Body

1 Eat breakfast.

2 Start an exercise program today and do it faithfully for thirty days. Walk, run, swim, bike, rollerblade, lift weights, etc. Choose something you really enjoy.

3 Give up a bad habit for a week. Go without alcohol, soda pop, fried foods, donuts, chocolate, or whatever else may be hurting your body. A week later, see how you feel.

Mind

4 Subscribe to a popular magazine that has some educational value, such as *Popular Mechanics* or *National Geographic*.

5 Read a newspaper every day. Pay special attention to the headline stories and the opinions page.

6 The next time you go on a date, visit a museum or eat at an ethnic restaurant you've never been to before. Expand your horizons.

Heart

7 Go on a one-on-one outing with a family member like your mom or your brother. Catch a ball game, see a movie, go shopping, or get an ice cream.

8 Begin today to build your humor collection. Cut out your favorite cartoons, buy hilarious movies, or start your own collection of great jokes. In no time, you'll have something to go to when you're feeling stressed.

Soul

9 Watch the sunset tonight or get up early to watch the sunrise.

10 If you haven't already done it, start keeping a journal today.

11 Take time each day to meditate, reflect upon your life, or pray. Do what works for you.

Which of the Baby Steps did I try, and what did I learn?

Keep Hope Alive!

K I D , Y O U ' L L M O V E M O U N T A I N S !

Keep Hope Alive (T)his workbook was written to help you through the difficult and tumultuous teenage years—to help you navigate through the jungle and give you hope to succeed! The hope is that you can move forward, kick an addiction, get out of an abusive relationship, establish lifelong habits of effectiveness, get organized, and lead a balanced life. That's not asking much, is it?

If after reading *The 7 Habits of Highly Effective Teens* and after completing this personal workbook you are feeling overwhelmed and don't know where to start, try doing some Baby Steps. Thumb back through this personal workbook and ask yourself, "Which one or two habits am I having the *most* difficult time living?"

Then choose just one or two things to work on. Write them down here.

1. _____

_____

2. _____

_____

3. _____

_____

> So be sure when you step.
> Step with care and great tact
> And remember that life's
> A Great Balancing Act.
>
> And will you succeed?
> Yes! You will, indeed!
> (98 and ¾ percent guaranteed)
> Kid, you'll move mountains.
>
> —DR. SEUSS
> FROM *OH, THE PLACES YOU'LL GO*

213

Start on those habits and you'll be amazed at the results you'll see in yourself after a few small changes. You're gonna feel more confident and happier—you'll experience a natural high. When you have that success, move on to the next.

The best way to internalize any of these habits is to share them with someone else while they're fresh on your mind.

I will share these ideas with the following person:

If you ever find yourself getting discouraged or falling short, remember that small adjustments have huge returns. Keep your hope alive!

Go for the best—you deserve it! And don't forget this great quote in the *Teens* book:

> You can't make footprints in the sands of time by sitting on your butt. And who wants to leave buttprints in the sands of time?
>
> —BOB MOAWAD

Write your own closing quote to a workbook just completed—and a journey just beginning:

Choose one or two Baby Steps you can do. Share your experiences with someone else or write your experiences and learnings here.

1 I will keep a journal of my innermost feelings, dreams, aspirations, and goals.

2 I will review this workbook and ask myself how I feel about the answers I gave. I will carefully review my life: Am I where I want to be, or am I on the right path to get to where I want to be?

3 I will memorize a quote that will help inspire me when I get discouraged.

4 I will keep hope alive! And I will help others keep hope alive, too.

Which of the Baby Steps did I try, and what did I learn?

About Franklin Covey

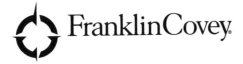

Franklin Covey Co. (NYSE: FC) is a global company specializing in performance improvement. We help organizations achieve results that require a change in human behavior. Our expertise is in seven areas: leadership, execution, productivity, trust, sales performance, customer loyalty, and education. Franklin Covey clients have included 90 percent of the Fortune 100, more than 75 percent of the Fortune 500, thousands of small- and mid-sized businesses, as well as numerous government entities and educational institutions. Franklin Covey has more than 40 direct and licensee offices providing professional services in more than 140 countries. For more information, visit www.franklincovey.com.

About the Author

Sean Covey is executive vice president of Global Solutions and Partnerships for FranklinCovey and has led the development of most of FranklinCovey's organizational offerings, including: *Focus, Leadership, The 4 Disciplines of Execution, The Leader in Me,* and *The 7 Habits of Highly Effective People.* Sean oversees all of Franklin Covey's international partnerships, which cover more than 140 countries.

Sean is also FranklinCovey's Education Practice Leader and is devoted to transforming education around the globe through bringing leadership principles and skills to as many kids, educators, and schools as possible.

He is a *New York Times* bestselling author and has written several books, including *The 6 Most Important Decisions You'll Ever Make, The 7 Habits of Happy Kids, The 4 Disciplines of Execution,* and *The 7 Habits of Highly Effective Teens,* which has been translated into twenty languages and sold more than five million copies worldwide.

He is a seasoned speaker to kids, teens, and adults and has appeared on numerous radio and TV shows.

Sean graduated with honors from Brigham Young University with a bachelor's degree in English and later earned his MBA from Harvard Business School. As the starting quarterback for BYU, he led his team to two bowl games and was twice selected as the ESPN Most Valuable Player of the Game.

Born in Belfast Ireland, Sean's favorite activities include going to movies, working out, hanging out with his kids, riding his dirt bike, and writing poor poetry. Sean and his wife Rebecca live with their children in the Rocky Mountains.

For more information on Sean, visit www.seancovey.com.

Follow Sean on Twitter: www.twitter.com/sean_covey

Right now, my worst habits are:

The reason I have these bad habits is:

I've had these bad habits for (days, weeks, years?):

The bad results I get from having these bad habits are: (For example: I keep texting during class, which means I don't take notes and get lower grades then I should.)

From my list of bad habits above, the one habit I would like to change the most is:

Change the Bad to Good

On the table below, fill in the habits that you named above. Keep this table handy during the upcoming week and use it as a tool to help you remember to change your bad habits to good ones.

BAD HABIT I WANT TO CHANGE	GOOD HABIT I WANT TO REPLACE IT WITH

In School:

1. _____   1. _____
2. _____   2. _____
3. _____   3. _____

With My Family:

1. _____   1. _____
2. _____   2. _____
3. _____   3. _____

With My Friends:

1. _____   1. _____
2. _____   2. _____
3. _____   3. _____

Other:

1. _____   1. _____
2. _____   2. _____
3. _____   3. _____

A cool thing about the 7 Habits is how they build on each other. It's a progression—just like learning arithmetic before calculus, memorizing the alphabet before learning to spell, or programming a website before launching it online. Trees grow this way, too; they put down solid roots before the trunk, branches, or leaves begin to grow.

Fill in the habits on the tree that follows from what you have learned so far.

The Leader in Me™

Does Your School Empower Every Student to Be a Leader?

The Leader in Me is a schoolwide model that equips students with the leadership and life skills necessary to succeed in the twenty-first century. *Leader in Me* schools seamlessly integrate the 7 Habits and other leadership development into daily curriculum, activities, and culture. Through this approach, students learn to set and achieve meaningful goals, take responsibility for their learning, work well with others, and use their individual talents to better the school community.

"We only get one chance to prepare our students for a future none of us can possibly predict. What are we going to do with that one chance?"

- Muriel Summers

www.TheLeaderinMe.org | 1-800-272-6839

FranklinCovey | EDUCATION

The Leader in Me™

Key skills business leaders have identified as vital to the futures of today's students are developed within *The Leader in Me* process.

- Leadership
- Accountability
- Adaptability
- Initiative and Self Direction
- Cross-Cultural Skills
- Responsibility
- Problem Solving
- Creativity
- Teamwork

"We're seeing trends in improvements, with attendance at an all-time high and discipline problems at an all-time low. We're becoming a lighthouse to the community, too, reaching out to our neighbors. Leader in Me isn't a curriculum or program, it's a total shift in school culture, one that teachers and students have fully embraced. These students are our future..."

- Jennie Hoke, Principal, FL

RESULTS

- Academic Achievement
- Student Self-Confidence
- Parent Involvement
- Discipline Referrals
- Staff Turnover

Partner with FranklinCovey to bring *The Leader in Me* to schools in your community...

www.TheLeaderinMe.org | 1-800-272-6839

FranklinCovey | EDUCATION

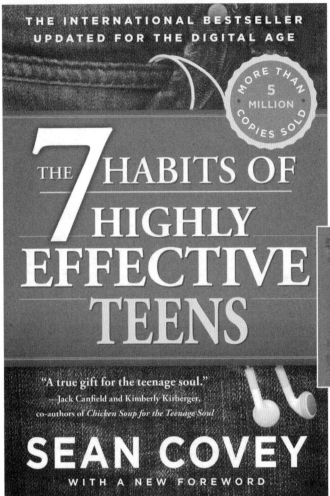